BEST OF THE CLASH

Music transcriptions by Steve Gorenberg, Jeff Perrin, and Dave Whitehill

Photos by Bob Gruen/STAR FILE

ISBN 0-7935-6996-6

HAL•LEONARD® CORPORATION

7777 W. BLUEMOUND RD. P.O. BOX 13819 MILWAUKEE, WI 53213

Visit Hal Leonard Online at
www.halleonard.com

BEST OF THE CLASH

CONTENTS

from *The Clash*

Career Opportunities

Words and Music by Joe Strummer and Mick Jones

Clampdown

Words and Music by Joe Strummer and Mick Jones

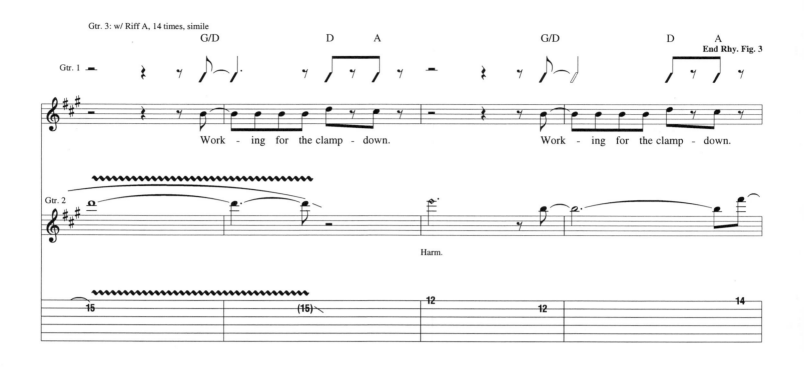

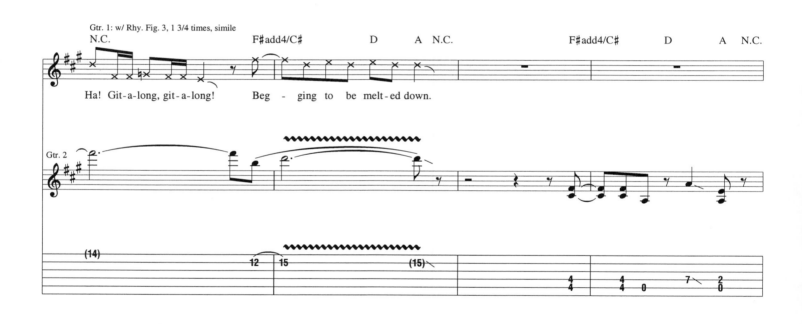

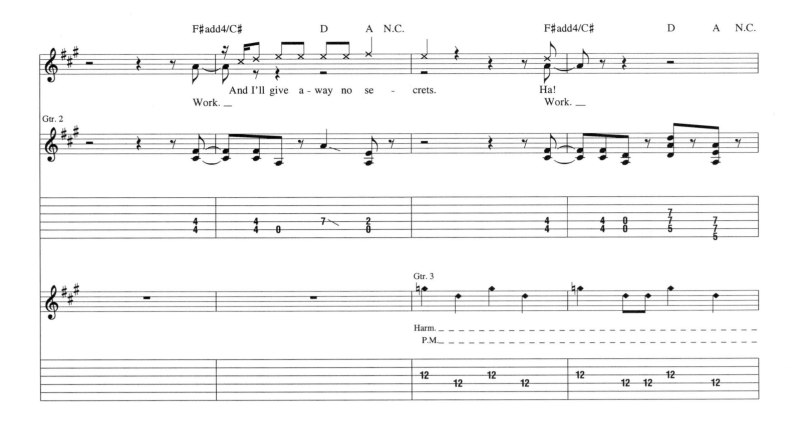

* composite arrangement

Clash City Rockers

Words and Music by Joe Strummer and Mick Jones

20

from *The Clash*

Complete Control

Words and Music by Joe Strummer and Mick Jones

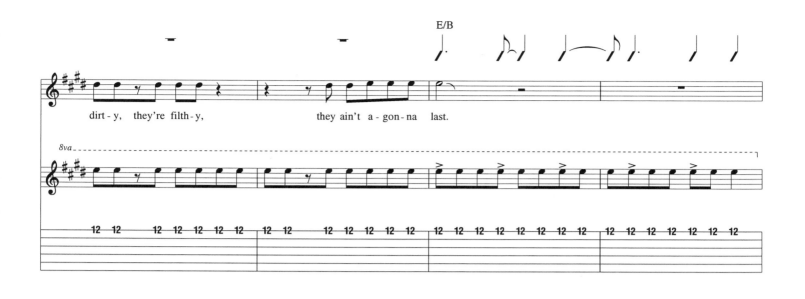

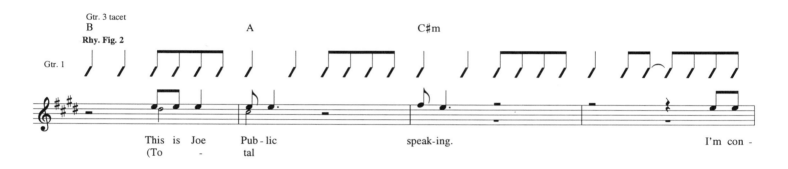

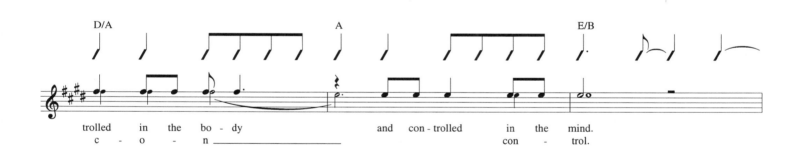

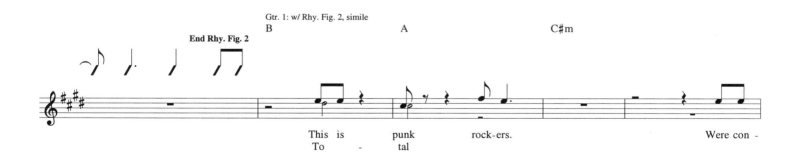

Outro-Guitar Solo

Gtr. 1: w/ Rhy. Fig. 2, 3 3/4 times

26

from *The Clash—On Broadway*

48 Hours

Words and Music by Joe Strummer and Mick Jones

Guitar Solo

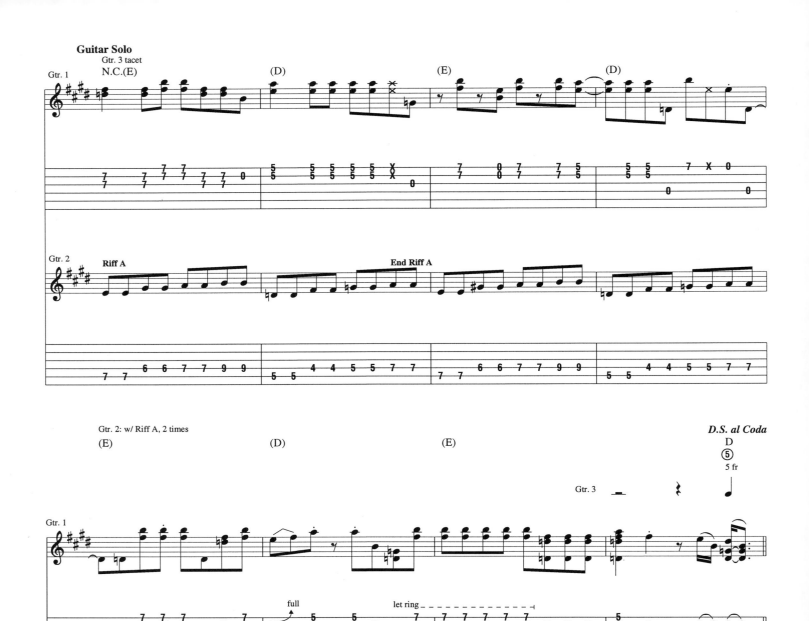

Ghetto Defendant

Words and Music by Joe Strummer and Mick Jones

Additional Lyrics

(...jiffy.)

3. Ghetto defendant, it is heroin pity.
   (Strung out committee.)
   Not tear gas, nor baton charge,
   Will stop you taking the city.
   (Not sitting pretty.)
   Heroin pity.
   (Graphed in a jiffy.)
   Not tear gas, nor baton charge,
   Will stop you taking the city.
   The ghetto prince of gutter poets was bounced out of the room.
   (Jean Arthur and Rambo.)
   By the bodyguards of greed, for disturbing the tomb.
   His words like flamethrowers, burnt the ghettos in their chests.
   (Eighteen-seventy-three, Paris commune.)
   His face painted whiter, and he was laid to rest.

4. Ghetto defendant, it is heroin pity.
   (Died in Marseille, buried in Charleville.)
   Not tear gas, nor baton charge,
   Stops you taking the city.
   (Shot into eternity.)
   It is heroin pity.
   Not tear gas, nor baton charge,
   Stops you taking the city.
   (Guatemala, Honduras, Poland, Hundred Years War.)
   (TV re-run invasion, Death Squad Salvador.)
   (Afghanistan, Meditation, Old Chinese flu.)
   (Kick junk, what else can a poor worker do?)

Know Your Rights

Words and Music by Joe Strummer and Mick Jones

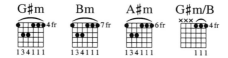

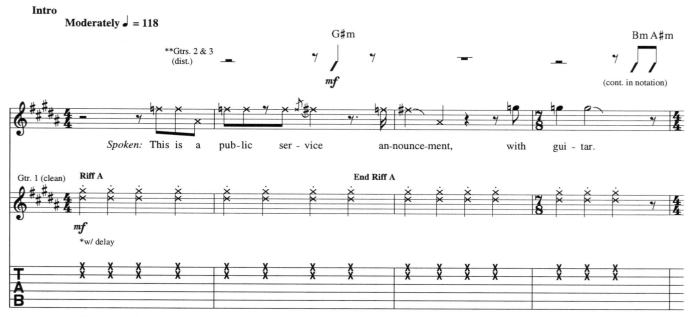

*Delay set for sixteenth note triplet regeneration, with 5 repeats.
**composite arrangement

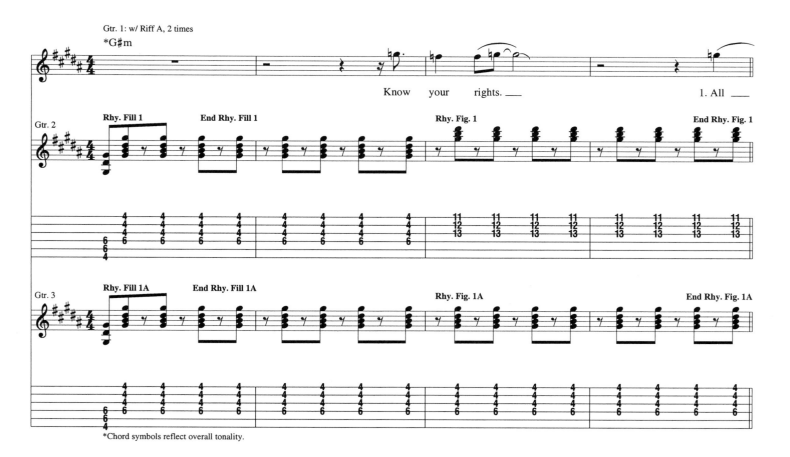

*Chord symbols reflect overall tonality.

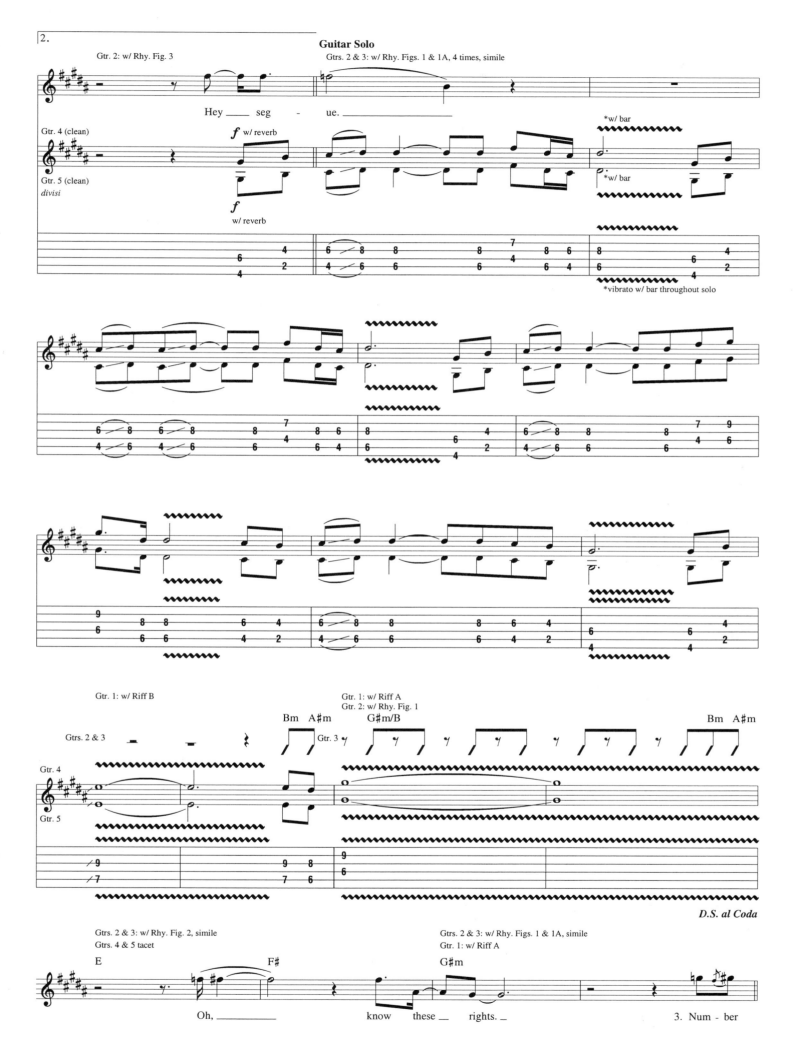

London Calling

Words and Music by Joe Strummer and Mick Jones

Gtr. 1: w/ Rhy. Fig. 2, simile

London calling to the underworld. Come out of the cupboard, you boys and girls.

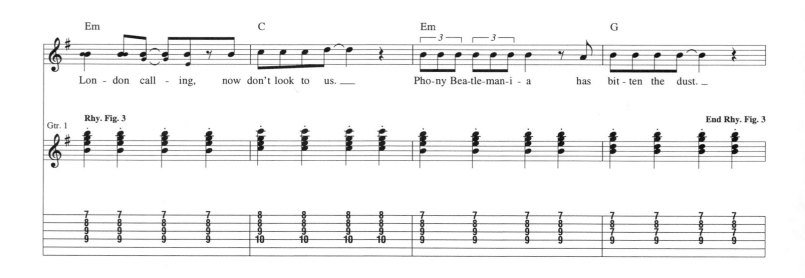

London calling, now don't look to us. Phony Beatlemania has bitten the dust.

Rhy. Fig. 3

Gtr. 1

End Rhy. Fig. 3

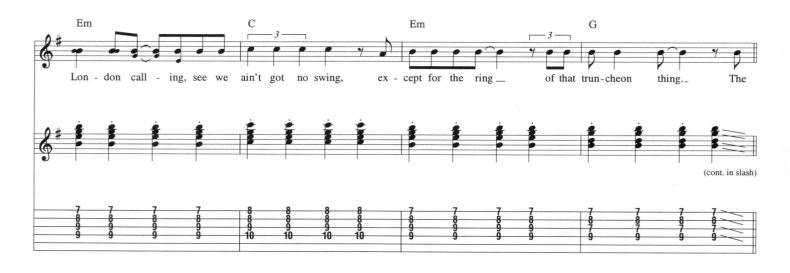

London calling, see we ain't got no swing, except for the ring of that truncheon thing. The

(cont. in slash)

Chorus

Rhy. Fig. 4

Gtr. 1

ice age is coming, the sun's zooming in. Meltdown expected, the

Rhy. Fig. 4A

Gtrs. 2 & 3

wheat is ___ grow-ing thin. En - gines stop run - ning, but I have no fear, 'cos

Lon - don is drown-ing and ___ I ___ live by the riv - er. ___

End Rhy. Fig. 4

End Rhy. Fig. 4A

Verse
Gtr. 1: w/ Rhy. Fig. 3, 2 times, simile

(Lon - don call - ing.) 2. To the im - i - ta - tion zone. For-get it, broth-er, you can go it a - lone. __

Gtr. 3

fdbk.

Gtr. 2

fdbk.

Gtrs. 2 & 3 tacet

Lon - don call - ing to the zom-bies of death, _ quit hold-ing out and draw an-oth-er breath. _

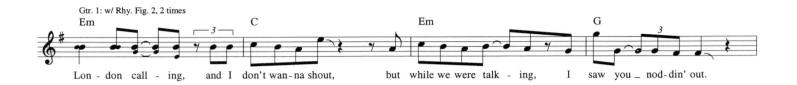

Gtr. 1: w/ Rhy. Fig. 2, 2 times

Lon - don call - ing, and I don't wan-na shout, but while we were talk - ing, I saw you _ nod-din' out.

Lon - don call - ing, see we ain't got no highs, ex - cept for that one with the yel - low - y eyes. The

Chorus
Gtr. 1: w/ Rhy. Fig. 4
Gtrs. 2 & 3: w/ Rhy. Fig. 4A, simile

ice age is com-ing, the sun's zoom-ing in. _ En - gines stop run-ning, the wheat is _ grow-ing thin. A

nu - cle - ar er - ror, but I have no fear, 'cos Lon - don is drown-ing and _ I _

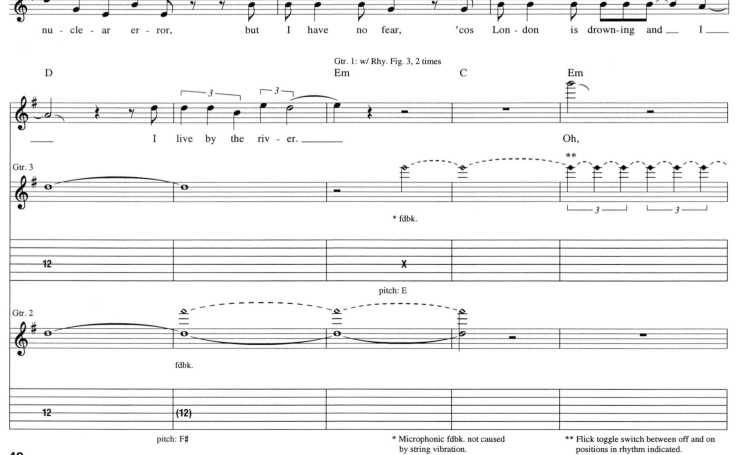

Gtr. 1: w/ Rhy. Fig. 3, 2 times

_ I live by the riv - er. _____ Oh,

* fdbk.

pitch: E

pitch: F#

* Microphonic fdbk. not caused by string vibration.

** Flick toggle switch between off and on positions in rhythm indicated.

42

Interlude

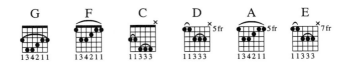

from *The Clash*

London's Burning

Words and Music by Joe Strummer and Mick Jones

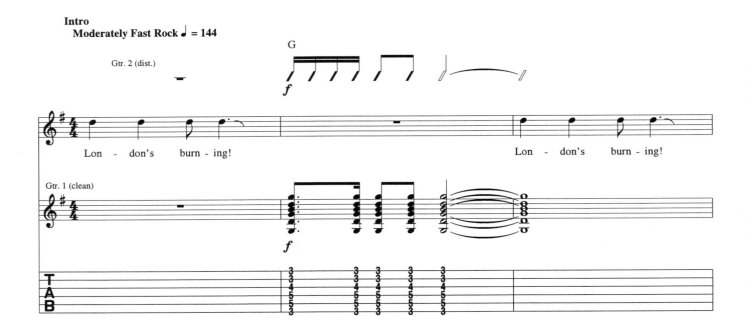

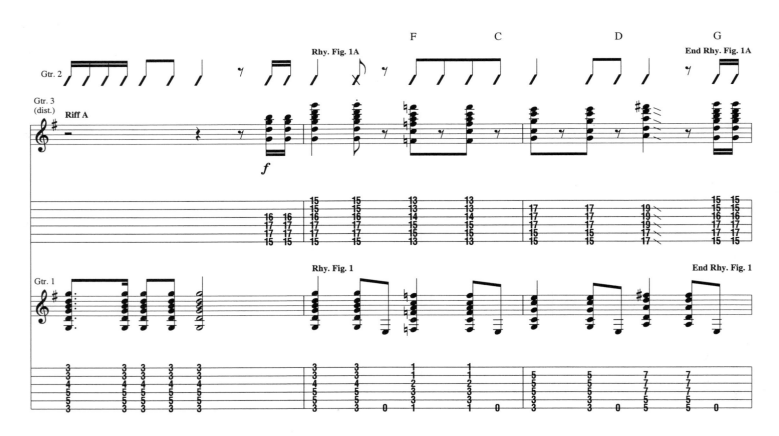

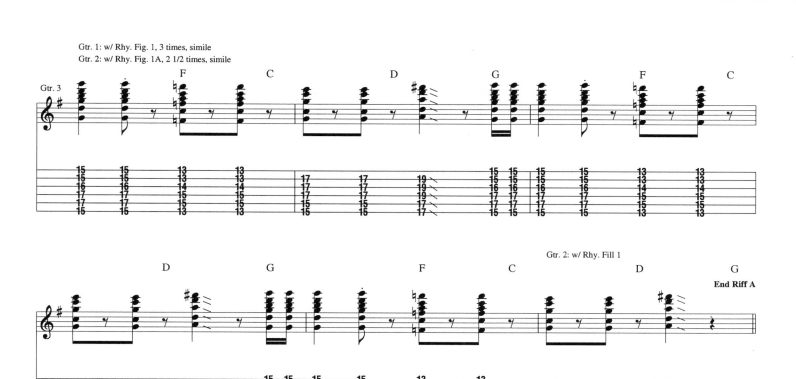

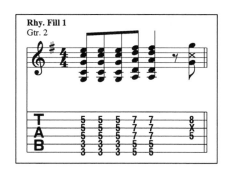

Black or white, ya turn it on, ya face the new re-lig-ion. Ev-'ry-bod-y's sit-ting 'round, watch-ing tel-e-vi-sion!

Gtr. 3: w/ Riff A

full

(cont. in slash)

End Rhy. Fig. 2

Chorus

Gtr. 1: w/ Rhy. Fig. 1, 4 times, simile

Gtr. 2: w/ Rhy. Fig. 1B, 3 times, simile

Rhy. Fig. 1B

End Rhy. Fig. 1B

Gtr. 2

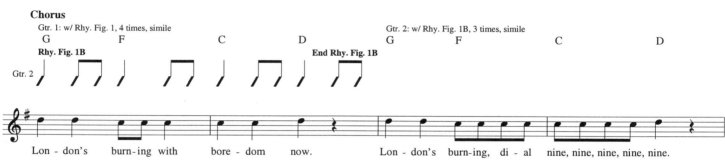

Lon - don's burn-ing with bore - dom now. Lon - don's burn-ing, di - al nine, nine, nine, nine, nine.

Lon - don's burn-ing with bore - dom now. Lon - don's burn-ing, di - al nine, nine, nine, nine, nine. 2. I'm

Verse

Gtr. 1: w/ Rhy. Fig. 2

up and down the west-way, in an' out the light. What a great traf-fic sys-tem; it's so bright. I

Gtr. 2

48

Outro-Guitar Solo

Lon-don's burn-ing.

pitch: F   B

51

The Magnificent Seven

Words and Music by Joe Strummer, Mick Jones and Topper Headon

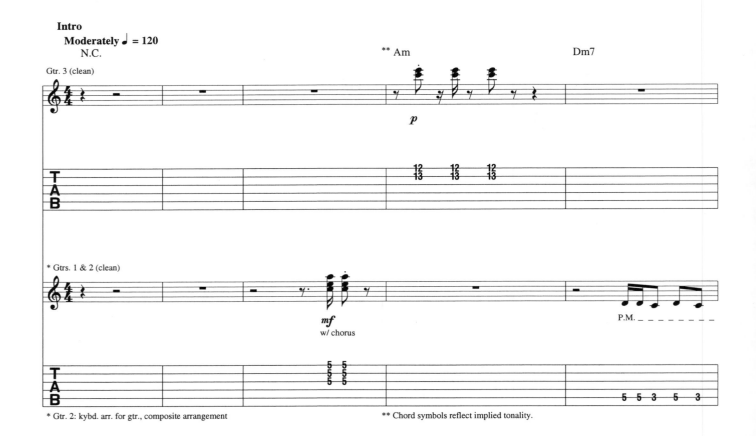

* Gtr. 2: kybd. arr. for gtr., composite arrangement

** Chord symbols reflect implied tonality.

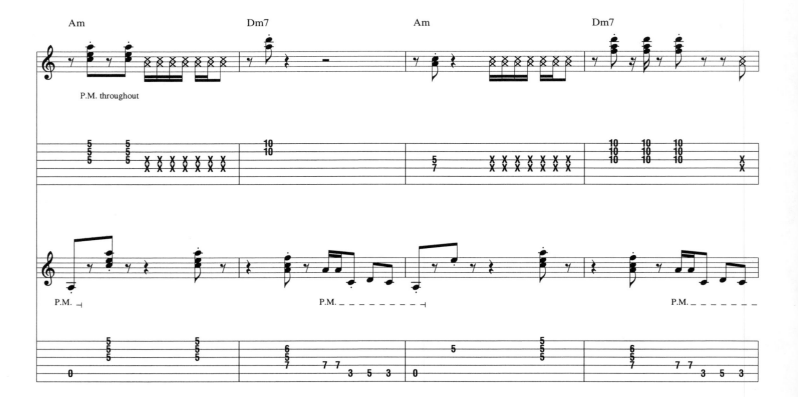

Shout: The Mag-nif - i - cent   Sev-en.

* Gtr. 2 to left of slash in TAB.

** Gtr. 2 to left of slash in TAB.

from *The Clash—Combat Rock*

Rock the Casbah

Words and Music by Joe Strummer, Mick Jones and Topper Headon

riff _____ don't like it. _____   Rock-in' the Cas - bah,   rock   the Cas - bah. 2. By

rock   the Cas - bah.   Now   o - ver   at   the   tem - ple.   Oh!   They

real - ly pack 'em in. _____   The   in - crowd _____ say it's _____ cool

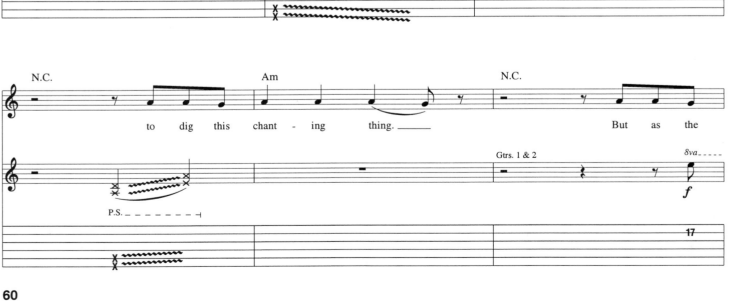

to   dig   this   chant - ing   thing. _____   But   as   the

soon as the Sha - riff was chauf-feured out - ta there, the jet pi - lots tuned _ to the cock-pit ra - di - o blare. As

soon as the sha - riff was out - ta their hair, the jet pi - lots wailed. _____ Sha -

Chorus

riff _____ don't like it. _____ Rock - in' the Cas - bah, rock the Cas - bah. Sha -

riff _____ don't like it. _____ Rock - in' the Cas - bah, rock the Cas - bah.
(Sha -

He thinks it's not ko - sher. Rock - in' the Cas - bah,

rock the Cas - bah. Sha - riff _____ don't _ like it. ____ Fun - da - men - tal - ly can't take it.

Begin Fade

Rock - in' the Cas - bah, rock the Cas - bah. Sha - riff _____ don't _ like it. ____ You know he real - ly hates it.

Fade Out

Rock - in' the Cas - bah, rock the Cas - bah. Sha - riff _____ don't _ like it. ____) Real - ly, real - ly hates it.

62

Safe European Home

Words and Music by Joe Strummer and Mick Jones

** Bkgd. Voc. doubled one octave lower throughout Verse.

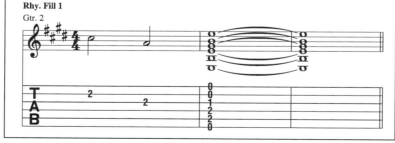

66

Outro

Gtrs. 1 & 2: w/ Rhy. Fig. 2, 3 times
*** Gtr. 3: w/ Rhy. Fig. 2A, 3 times

*** Gtr. 3, Bass & Drums fade in, 1st 4 meas.

Additional Lyrics

3. They got the sun, an' they got the palm trees.
   They got the weed, an' they got the taxis.
   Whoa, the harder they come, n' the home of ol' bluebeat.
   Yes I'd stay an' be a tourist, but I can't take the gunplay.

Should I Stay or Should I Go

Words and Music by Joe Strummer and Mick Jones

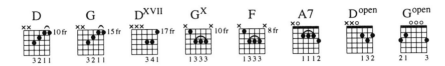

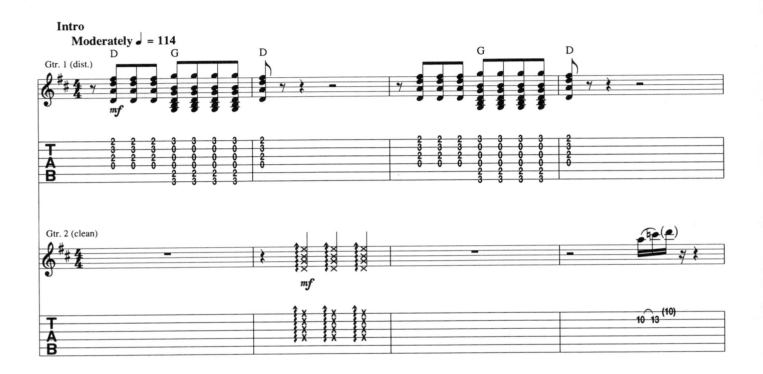

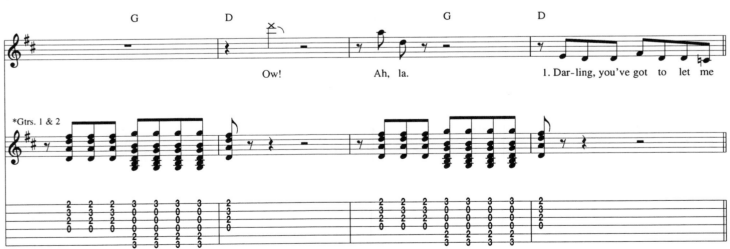

*composite arrangement

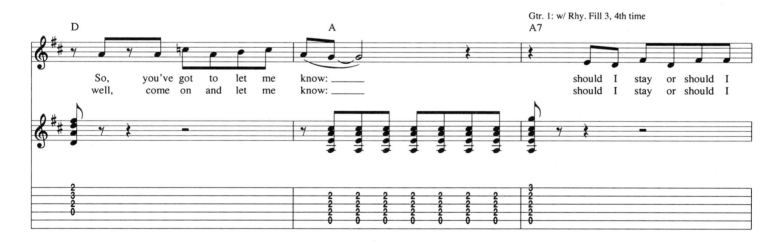

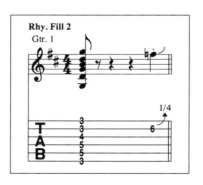

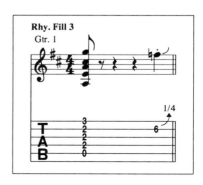

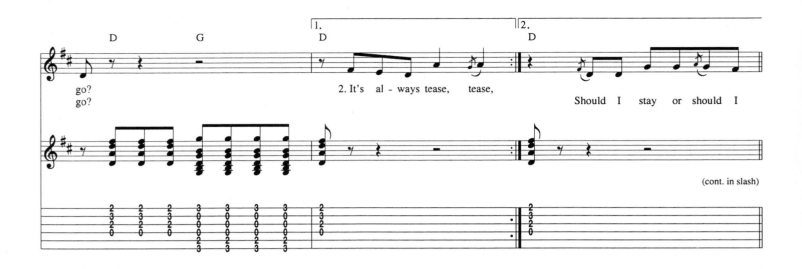

go?
go?

2. It's al-ways tease, tease,

Should I stay or should I

(cont. in slash)

Chorus
Double-Time Feel

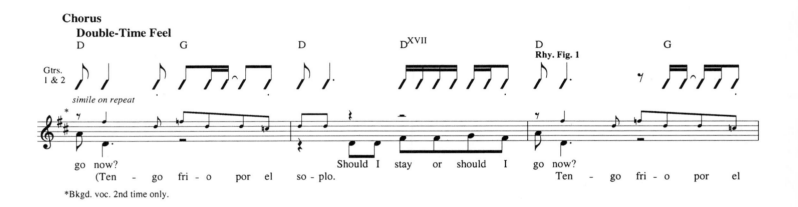

go now?
(Ten - go fri - o por el so - plo.

*Bkgd. voc. 2nd time only.

Should I stay or should I go now?

Ten - go fri - o por el

If I go, there will be trou-ble,
so - plo. Si me voy - va a ser pe-li - gro.

and if I stay, it will be

To Coda

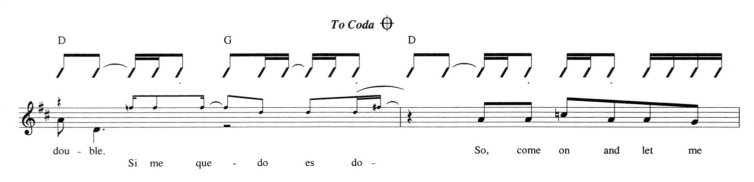

dou - ble.
Si me que - do es do -

So, come on and let me

End Double-Time Feel

End Rhy. Fig. 1

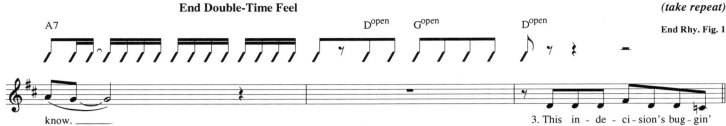

know. ____

3. This in - de - ci - sion's bug - gin'

⊕ *Coda*

So, you've got to let me know: ____

should I cool it or should I

- ble.

Me ti - en - es que de - cir.

Outro-Chorus
Gtrs. 1 & 2: w/ Rhy. Fig. 1, simile

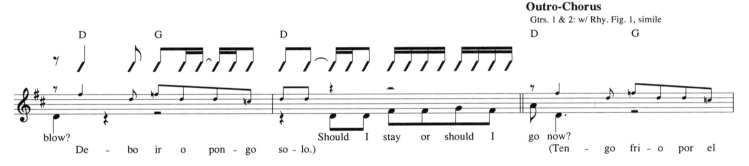

blow?

De - bo ir o pon - go so - lo.)

Should I stay or should I go now?

(Ten - go fri - o por el

so - plo.

If I go, there will be trou - ble,

Si me voy ____ va a ser pe - li - gro.

and if I stay, it will be

dou - ble.

Si me que - do ____ es do - ble.

So, you've got to let me know: ____

Me ti - en - es que de -

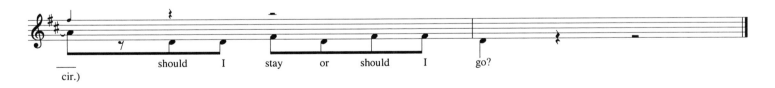

cir.)

should I stay or should I go?

Additional Lyrics

3. This indecision's buggin' me. *(Indecisión me molesta.)*
   If you don't want me, set me free. *(Si no me quieres líbrame.)*
   Exactly who I'm s'pose to be? *(Dígame que tengo ser.)*
   Don't you know which clothes even fit me? *(Sabes que ropa me queda?)*
   Come on and let me know: *(Me tienes que decir.)*
   Should I cool it or should I blow? *(Me debo ir o quedarme?)*

4. *Instrumental (w/ Voc. ad lib.)*

Straight to Hell

Words and Music by Joe Strummer, Mick Jones, Paul Simonon and Topper Headon

ice, this is your ___ par - a - dise. There ain't no

End Rhy. Fig. 2

Chorus
Gtr. 1: w/ Riff A, simile

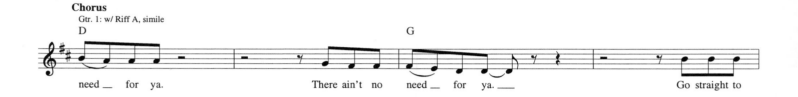

need ___ for ya. There ain't no need ___ for ya. ___ Go straight to

Gtr. 2: w/ Rhy. Fill 1

hell, ___ boys. ___ Go straight to hell, ___ boys.

Verse
Gtr. 1: w/ Rhy. Fig. 2

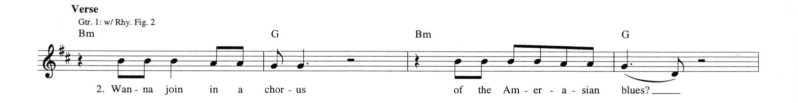

2. Wan - na join in a chor - us of the Am - er - a - sian blues? ___

When it's ___ Christ - mas out in Ho Chi Minh ___ Cit - y, Kid - die say, "Pa - pa, Pa - pa, Pa - pa, Pa - pa, Pa - pa - san, ___

___ take me home. ___ See me ___ got pho - to, pho - to, pho - to - graph of you and

Ma - ma, Ma - ma, Ma - ma - san, of you and Ma - ma, Ma - ma, Ma - ma - san." Lem - me tell ya 'bout your

74

Train in Vain

Words and Music by Joe Strummer and Mick Jones

Outro

Play 4 Times and Fade

Additional Lyrics

3. Now, I've got a job, but it don't pay.
   I need new clothes, I need someone to save.
   But without all of these things I can do,
   But without your love, I won't make it through.
   But you don't understand my point of view,
   I suppose there's nothing I can do.

from *The Clash*

White Man in Hammersmith Palais

Words and Music by Joe Strummer and Mick Jones

*Rhy. Fill 1 refers to Gtr. 4 only.

first time _ from Ja - mai - ca.
fool - ing _ with your guns. _
They won't no-tice an - y-way. _

Dil - lin - ger _ and
The Brit - ish ar - my _ is

Gtr. 3: w/ Fill 1, 2nd & 3rd times

Le - roy Smart, Del - roy Wil - son, your cool op - er - a - tor.
wait-ing out there, it weighs _ fif - teen hun - dred tons. _
fight - ing, for a good place un - der the light - ing. _ The

End Rhy. Fig. 1

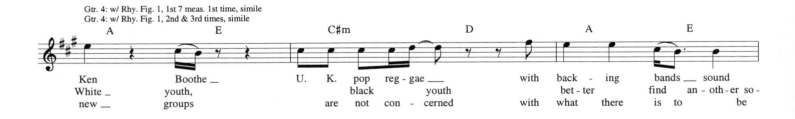

Gtr. 4: w/ Rhy. Fig. 1, 1st 7 meas. 1st time, simile
Gtr. 4: w/ Rhy. Fig. 1, 2nd & 3rd times, simile

Ken Boothe _ U. K. pop reg - gae _ with back - ing bands _ sound
White _ youth, black youth bet - ter find an - oth - er so -
new _ groups are not con - cerned with what there is to be

Voc. Fig. 2

Ah, _ ah, _ ah. _

Fill 1
Gtr. 3

Coda 2

White Riot

Words and Music by Joe Strummer and Mick Jones

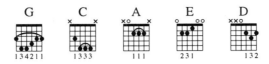

*Two gtrs. arr. for one.

*bass plays C#

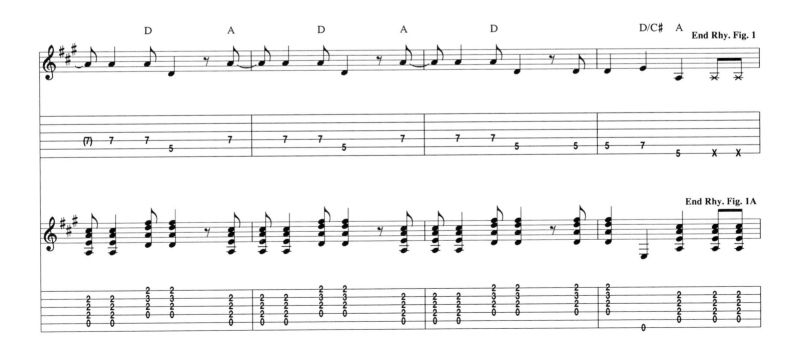

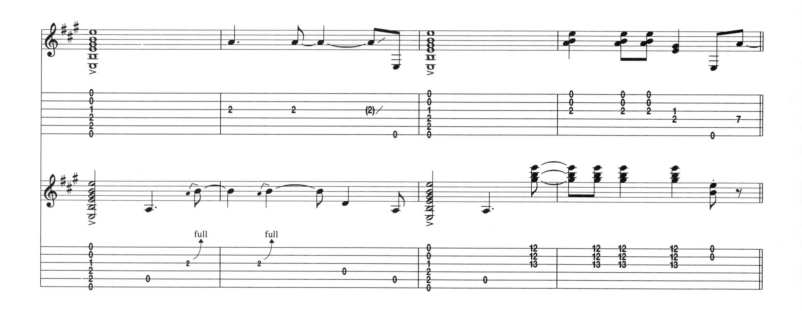

𝄋 **Chorus**

Gtrs. 1 & 2: w/ Rhy. Figs. 1 & 1A, simile

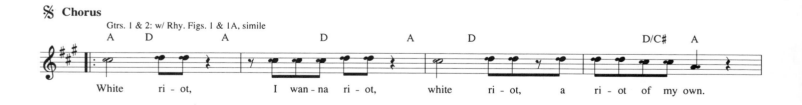

White ri-ot, I wan-na ri-ot, white ri-ot, a ri-ot of my own.

To Coda ⊕

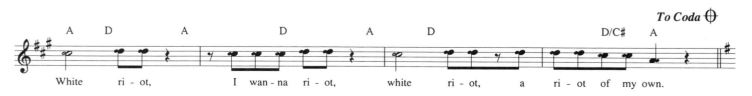

White ri-ot, I wan-na ri-ot, white ri-ot, a ri-ot of my own.

Verse

no-bod-y wants   to go to jail.

Guitar Solo

D.S. al Coda

⊕ *Coda*
Bridge

Gtr. 1

Are you tak-ing o-ver,   or are you tak-ing or-ders?

Gtr. 2

Are you go - in' back - wards, or are you go - in' for - wards?

Outro-Chorus

Gtrs. 1 & 2: w/ Rhy. Figs. 1 & 1A, 1st 4 meas., simile

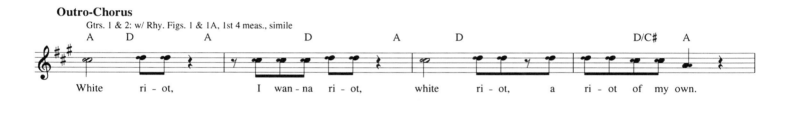

White ri - ot, I wan - na ri - ot, white ri - ot, a ri - ot of my own.

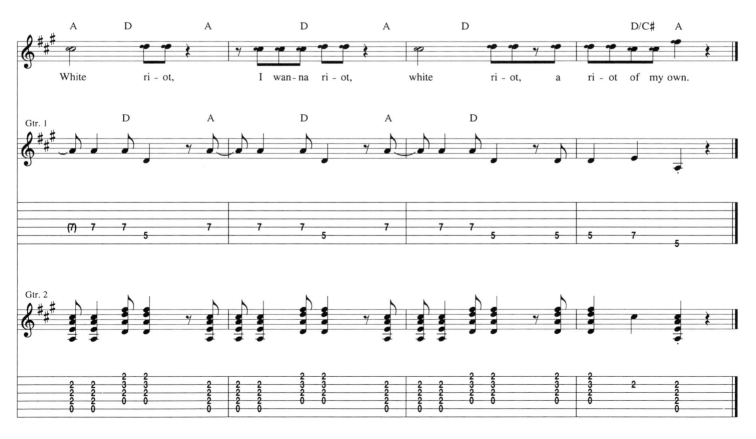

White ri - ot, I wan - na ri - ot, white ri - ot, a ri - ot of my own.

Guitar Notation Legend

Guitar Music can be notated three different ways: on a *musical staff*, in *tablature*, and in *rhythm slashes*.

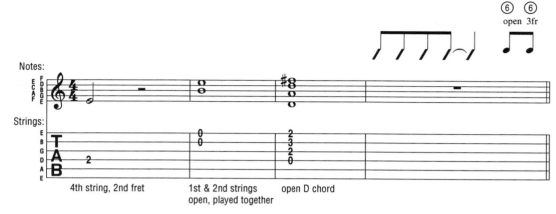

RHYTHM SLASHES are written above the staff. Strum chords in the rhythm indicated. Use the chord diagrams found at the top of the first page of the transcription for the appropriate chord voicings. Round noteheads indicate single notes.

THE MUSICAL STAFF shows pitches and rhythms and is divided by bar lines into measures. Pitches are named after the first seven letters of the alphabet.

TABLATURE graphically represents the guitar fingerboard. Each horizontal line represents a a string, and each number represents a fret.

4th string, 2nd fret   1st & 2nd strings open, played together   open D chord

Definitions for Special Guitar Notation

HALF-STEP BEND: Strike the note and bend up 1/2 step.

WHOLE-STEP BEND: Strike the note and bend up one step.

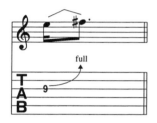

GRACE NOTE BEND: Strike the note and bend up as indicated. The first note does not take up any time.

SLIGHT (MICROTONE) BEND: Strike the note and bend up 1/4 step.

BEND AND RELEASE: Strike the note and bend up as indicated, then release back to the original note. Only the first note is struck.

PRE-BEND: Bend the note as indicated, then strike it.

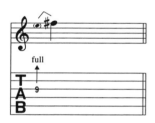

PRE-BEND AND RELEASE: Bend the note as indicated. Strike it and release the bend back to the original note.

UNISON BEND: Strike the two notes simultaneously and bend the lower note up to the pitch of the higher.

VIBRATO: The string is vibrated by rapidly bending and releasing the note with the fretting hand.

WIDE VIBRATO: The pitch is varied to a greater degree by vibrating with the fretting hand.

HAMMER-ON: Strike the first (lower) note with one finger, then sound the higher note (on the same string) with another finger by fretting it without picking.

PULL-OFF: Place both fingers on the notes to be sounded. Strike the first note and without picking, pull the finger off to sound the second (lower) note.

LEGATO SLIDE: Strike the first note and then slide the same fret-hand finger up or down to the second note. The second note is not struck.

SHIFT SLIDE: Same as legato slide, except the second note is struck.

TRILL: Very rapidly alternate between the notes indicated by continuously hammering on and pulling off.

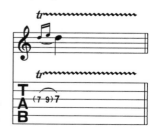

TAPPING: Hammer ("tap") the fret indicated with the pick-hand index or middle finger and pull off to the note fretted by the fret hand.

NATURAL HARMONIC: Strike the note while the fret-hand lightly touches the string directly over the fret indicated.

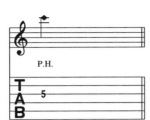

PINCH HARMONIC: The note is fretted normally and a harmonic is produced by adding the edge of the thumb or the tip of the index finger of the pick hand to the normal pick attack.

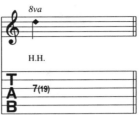

HARP HARMONIC: The note is fretted normally and a harmonic is produced by gently resting the pick hand's index finger directly above the indicated fret (in parentheses) while the pick hand's thumb or pick assists by plucking the appropriate string.

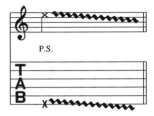

PICK SCRAPE: The edge of the pick is rubbed down (or up) the string, producing a scratchy sound.

MUFFLED STRINGS: A percussive sound is produced by laying the fret hand across the string(s) without depressing, and striking them with the pick hand.

PALM MUTING: The note is partially muted by the pick hand lightly touching the string(s) just before the bridge.

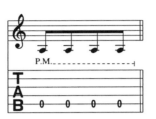

RAKE: Drag the pick across the strings indicated with a single motion.

TREMOLO PICKING: The note is picked as rapidly and continuously as possible.

ARPEGGIATE: Play the notes of the chord indicated by quickly rolling them from bottom to top.

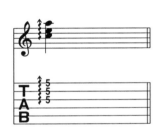

VIBRATO BAR DIVE AND RETURN: The pitch of the note or chord is dropped a specified number of steps (in rhythm) then returned to the original pitch.

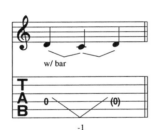

VIBRATO BAR SCOOP: Depress the bar just before striking the note, then quickly release the bar.

VIBRATO BAR DIP: Strike the note and then immediately drop a specified number of steps, then release back to the original pitch.

Additional Musical Definitions

 (accent) • Accentuate note (play it louder)

 (accent) • Accentuate note with great intensity

 (staccato) • Play the note short

⊓ • Downstroke

∨ • Upstroke

D.S. al Coda • Go back to the sign (𝄋), then play until the measure marked "***To Coda***," then skip to the section labelled "***Coda***."

D.S. al Fine • Go back to the beginning of the song and play until the measure marked "***Fine***" (end).

Rhy. Fig. • Label used to recall a recurring accompaniment pattern (usually chordal).

Riff • Label used to recall composed, melodic lines (usually single notes) which recur.

Fill • Label used to identify a brief melodic figure which is to be inserted into the arrangement.

Rhy. Fill • A chordal version of a Fill.

tacet • Instrument is silent (drops out).

 • Repeat measures between signs.

 • When a repeated section has different endings, play the first ending only the first time and the second ending only the second time.

NOTE: Tablature numbers in parentheses mean:
1. The note is being sustained over a system (note in standard notation is tied), or
2. The note is sustained, but a new articulation (such as a hammer-on, pull-off, slide or vibrato begins, or
3. The note is a barely audible "ghost" note (note in standard notation is also in parentheses).

RECORDED VERSIONS
GUITAR
The Best Note-For-Note Transcriptions Available

ALL BOOKS INCLUDE TABLATURE

00690199 Aerosmith – Nine Lives $19.95	00690068 Return Of The Hellecasters $19.95	00690090 Red Hot Chili Peppers – One Hot Minute ..$22.95
00690146 Aerosmith – Toys in the Attic $19.95	00692930 Jimi Hendrix – Are You Experienced? $24.95	00694892 Guitar Style Of Jerry Reed $19.95
00694865 Alice In Chains – Dirt $19.95	00692931 Jimi Hendrix – Axis: Bold As Love $22.95	00694937 Jimmy Reed – Master Bluesman $19.95
00694932 Allman Brothers Band – Volume 1 ......$24.95	00692932 Jimi Hendrix – Electric Ladyland $24.95	00694899 R.E.M. – Automatic For The People $19.95
00694933 Allman Brothers Band – Volume 2 ......$24.95	00690218 Jimi Hendrix – First Rays of the New Rising Sun $24.95	00690260 Jimmie Rodgers Guitar Collection $17.95
00694934 Allman Brothers Band – Volume 3 ......$24.95	00690038 Gary Hoey – Best Of $19.95	00690014 Rolling Stones – Exile On Main Street ...$24.95
00694877 Chet Atkins – Guitars For All Seasons ...$19.95	00660029 Buddy Holly $19.95	00690186 Rolling Stones – Rock & Roll Circus $19.95
00694918 Randy Bachman Collection $22.95	00660169 John Lee Hooker – A Blues Legend $19.95	00690135 Otis Rush Collection $19.95
00694880 Beatles – Abbey Road $19.95	00690054 Hootie & The Blowfish –	00690031 Santana's Greatest Hits $19.95
00694863 Beatles –	Cracked Rear View $19.95	00694805 Scorpions – Crazy World $19.95
Sgt. Pepper's Lonely Hearts Club Band ..$19.95	00694905 Howlin' Wolf $19.95	00690150 Son Seals – Bad Axe Blues $17.95
00690174 Beck – Mellow Gold $17.95	00690136 Indigo Girls – 1200 Curfews $22.95	00690128 Seven Mary Three – American Standards ..$19.95
00690346 Beck – Mutations $19.95	00694938 Elmore James –	00690076 Sex Pistols – Never Mind The Bollocks ..$19.95
00690175 Beck – Odelay $17.95	Master Electric Slide Guitar $19.95	00120105 Kenny Wayne Shepherd – Ledbetter Heights $19.95
00694884 The Best of George Benson $19.95	00690167 Skip James Blues Guitar Collection $16.95	00120123 Kenny Wayne Shepherd – Trouble Is $19.95
00692385 Chuck Berry $19.95	00694833 Billy Joel For Guitar $19.95	00690196 Silverchair – Freak Show $19.95
00692200 Black Sabbath –	00694912 Eric Johnson – Ah Via Musicom $19.95	00690130 Silverchair – Frogstomp $19.95
We Sold Our Soul For Rock 'N' Roll $19.95	00690169 Eric Johnson – Venus Isle $22.95	00690041 Smithereens – Best Of $19.95
00690115 Blind Melon – Soup $19.95	00694799 Robert Johnson – At The Crossroads ...$19.95	00694885 Spin Doctors – Pocket Full of Kryptonite ..$19.95
00690305 Blink 182 – Dude Ranch $19.95	00693185 Judas Priest – Vintage Hits $19.95	00690124 Sponge – Rotting Pinata $19.95
00690241 Bloodhound Gang – One Fierce Beer Coaster .$19.95	00690277 Best of Kansas $19.95	00120004 Steely Dan – Best Of $24.95
00690028 Blue Oyster Cult – Cult Classics $19.95	00690073 B. B. King – 1950-1957 ....$24.95	00694921 Steppenwolf, The Best Of $22.95
00690219 Blur $19.95	00690098 B. B. King – 1958-1967 ....$24.95	00694957 Rod Stewart – Acoustic Live $22.95
00694935 Boston: Double Shot Of $22.95	00690099 B. B. King – 1962-1971 ....$24.95	00690021 Sting – Fields Of Gold $19.95
00690237 Meredith Brooks – Blurring the Edges ..$19.95	00690134 Freddie King Collection $17.95	00120081 Sublime $19.95
00690168 Roy Buchanon Collection $19.95	00694903 The Best Of Kiss $24.95	00120122 Sublime – 40 Oz. to Freedom $19.95
00690337 Jerry Cantrell – Boggy Depot $19.95	00690157 Kiss – Alive $19.95	00690242 Suede – Coming Up $19.95
00690293 Best of Steven Curtis Chapman $19.95	00690163 Mark Knopfler/Chet Atkins – Neck and Neck $19.95	00694824 Best Of James Taylor $16.95
00690043 Cheap Trick – Best Of $19.95	00690296 Patty Larkin Songbook $17.95	00694887 Thin Lizzy – The Best Of Thin Lizzy $19.95
00120151 Best of the Chemical Brothers $14.95	00690202 Live – Secret Samadhi $19.95	00690238 Third Eye Blind $19.95
00690171 Chicago – Definitive Guitar Collection ...$22.95	00690070 Live – Throwing Copper $19.95	00690022 Richard Thompson Guitar $19.95
00660139 Eric Clapton – Journeyman $19.95	00690018 Living Colour – Best Of $19.95	00690267 311 ....$19.95
00694869 Eric Clapton – Live Acoustic $19.95	00694954 Lynyrd Skynyrd, New Best Of $19.95	00690030 Toad The Wet Sprocket $19.95
00694896 John Mayall/Eric Clapton – Bluesbreakers $19.95	00694845 Yngwie Malmsteen – Fire And Ice ...$19.95	00690228 Tonic – Lemon Parade $19.95
00690162 Best of the Clash $19.95	00694956 Bob Marley – Legend $19.95	00690295 Tool – Aenima $19.95
00690166 Albert Collins – The Alligator Years $16.95	00690283 Best of Sarah McLachlan $19.95	00694411 U2 – The Joshua Tree $19.95
00694940 Counting Crows – August & Everything After $19.95	00690239 Matchbox 20 – Yourself or Someone Like You .$19.95	00690039 Steve Vai – Alien Love Secrets $24.95
00690197 Counting Crows – Recovering the Satellites ..$19.95	00690244 Megadeath – Cryptic Writings $19.95	00690172 Steve Vai – Fire Garden $24.95
00690118 Cranberries – The Best of $19.95	00690236 Mighty Mighty Bosstones – Let's Face It ..$19.95	00690023 Jimmie Vaughan – Strange Pleasures ..$19.95
00690215 Music of Robert Cray $19.95	00690040 Steve Miller Band Greatest Hits $19.95	00660136 Stevie Ray Vaughan – In Step $19.95
00694840 Cream – Disraeli Gears $19.95	00690225 Moist – Creature $19.95	00694835 Stevie Ray Vaughan – The Sky Is Crying ..$19.95
00690007 Danzig 4 ....$19.95	00694802 Gary Moore – Still Got The Blues $19.95	00694776 Vaughan Brothers – Family Style $19.95
00690184 DC Talk – Jesus Freak $19.95	00690103 Alanis Morissette – Jagged Little Pill ..$19.95	00690217 Verve Pipe, The – Villains $19.95
00660186 Alex De Grassi Guitar Collection $19.95	00690341 Alanis Morisette –	00120026 Joe Walsh – Look What I Did... .....$24.95
00690289 Best of Deep Purple $17.95	Supposed Former Infatuation Junkie $19.95	00694789 Muddy Waters – Deep Blues $24.95
00694831 Derek And The Dominos –	00694958 Mountain, Best Of $19.95	00690071 Weezer $19.95
Layla & Other Assorted Love Songs $19.95	00694913 Nirvana – In Utero $19.95	00690286 Weezer – Pinkerton $19.95
00690322 Ani Di Franco – Little Plastic Castle $19.95	00694883 Nirvana – Nevermind $19.95	00694970 Who, The – Definitive Collection A-E ...$24.95
00690187 Dire Straits – Brothers In Arms $19.95	00690026 Nirvana – Acoustic In New York $19.95	00694971 Who, The – Definitive Collection F-Li ..$24.95
00690191 Dire Straits – Money For Nothing $24.95	00120112 No Doubt – Tragic Kingdom $22.95	00694972 Who, The – Definitive Collection Lo-R ..$24.95
00660178 Willie Dixon – Master Blues Composer ..$24.95	00690121 Oasis – (What's The Story) Morning Glory .$19.95	00694973 Who, The – Definitive Collection S-Y ..$24.95
00690250 Best of Duane Eddy $16.95	00690290 Offspring, The – Ignition $19.95	00690320 Best of Dar Williams $17.95
00690323 Fastball – All the Pain Money Can Buy ...$19.95	00690204 Offspring, The – Ixnay on the Hombre ..$17.95	00690319 Best of Stevie Wonder $19.95
00690089 Foo Fighters $19.95	00690203 Offspring, The – Smash $17.95	
00690235 Foo Fighters – The Colour and the Shape ..$19.95	00694830 Ozzy Osbourne – No More Tears $19.95	
00690042 Robben Ford Blues Collection $19.95	00694855 Pearl Jam – Ten $19.95	
00694920 Free – Best Of $18.95	00690053 Liz Phair – Whip Smart $19.95	
00690324 Fuel – Sunburn $19.95	00690176 Phish – Billy Breathes $22.95	
00690222 G3 Live – Satriani, Vai, Johnson $22.95	00690331 Phish – The Story of Ghost $19.95	
00694894 Frank Gambale – The Great Explorers ..$19.95	00693800 Pink Floyd – Early Classics $19.95	
00694807 Danny Gatton – 88 Elmira St $19.95	00694967 Police – Message In A Box Boxed Set ...$70.00	
00690127 Goo Goo Dolls – A Boy Named Goo ...$19.95	00690195 Presidents of the United States of America II $22.95	
00690338 Goo Goo Dolls – Dizzy Up the Girl ...$19.95	00694974 Queen – A Night At The Opera $19.95	
00690117 John Gorka Collection $19.95	00690145 Rage Against The Machine – Evil Empire ..$19.95	
00690114 Buddy Guy Collection Vol. A-J $22.95	00690179 Rancid – And Out Come the Wolves ..$22.95	
00690193 Buddy Guy Collection Vol. L-Y $22.95	00690055 Red Hot Chili Peppers –	
00694798 George Harrison Anthology $19.95	Bloodsugarsexmagik $19.95	

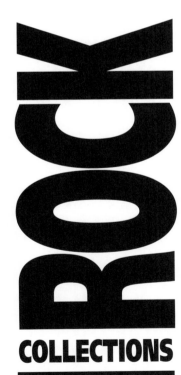